Animalographies

# Togo & Balto
## The Dogs Who Saved a Town

**Jodie Parachini**

illustrated by
**Keiron Ward** and **Jason Dewhirst**

Albert Whitman & Company
Chicago, Illinois

For Tom. Thank you for walking the dog—JP

For Mum, Audrey, and Dad, Keith.
Thanks for the gift of Art!—KW

Library of Congress Cataloging-in-Publication data is on file with the publisher.
Text copyright © 2022 by Jodie Parachini
Illustrations copyright © 2022 by Albert Whitman & Company
Illustrations by Keiron Ward and Jason Dewhirst
First published in the United States of America in 2022 by Albert Whitman & Company
ISBN 978-0-8075-0382-9 (hardcover) • ISBN 978-0-8075-0383-6 (ebook)

Printed in China
10 9 8 7 6 5 4 3 2 1 WKT 26 25 24 23 22 21
Design by Aphelandra
For more information about Albert Whitman & Company, visit our website at www.albertwhitman.com.

Hi! I'm Togo. I'm twelve years old. That's my friend Balto on the left. He's six.

Dogs are good at many things—fetching sticks, chasing cats, and digging enormous holes—but we can also be heroes! Some dogs assist soldiers in war or provide services for blind or disabled people, but we helped to save an entire town.

Balto and I are Siberian huskies.
And famous sled dogs.

What's a sled dog? For many years Alaska
Natives such as the Athabascans, Inuit, and
Yuit used dogs as pack animals to carry heavy
loads on their backs or to pull their owners'
belongings across the frozen ground.

By the early 1900s, when I was born, dogs were being harnessed to sleds to transport mail or people across parts of Alaska where trains couldn't go and where the newest form of transportation, the airplane, was unreliable, due to snowy weather conditions.

Balto and I learned to be sled dogs by the great trainer Leonhard Seppala (or "Sepp" to us dogs).

When I was a puppy, I was so small that Sepp gave me the name Cugu (pronounced like Togo), which means "puppy" in Northern Sami, the language spoken in the part of Norway where Sepp was born.

I didn't grow very big, and I was sick a lot as a young pup. No one ever thought I'd grow up to be famous.

Sepp tried to give me away when I was six months old because I was too mischievous! I was a rowdy rascal who was too playful with the other dogs. Sled dogs need to listen to instructions, which is something I didn't like to do, so I went to live with a neighbor to become a pet.

**TOGO'S DIARY 🐾 1913**

Today was an exciting day! Life as a pet is okay. I get lots of belly rubs and treats, but I miss the excitement of the kennel, where there is always barking and playing. So when no one was looking, I jumped through a window and went racing back to my old home. Boy was everyone surprised to see me!

Sepp kept me this time.
I was still rough and rowdy
but would immediately
settle down when he put
the harness on me, so Sepp
decided to try to train me
as a sled dog.

Turns out, I was amazing at it—I ran seventy-five miles on my first day with the sled; most puppies only manage a few miles.

Sepp called me a natural lead dog, though it took me a few years to get to that position. Lead dogs steer the team and set the pace. We must be intelligent and loyal, have great stamina, and be able to find the trail in bad conditions. When I was six, Balto was born, and Sepp trained him too. (Balto's the mostly black dog. He'll be a lead dog soon too.)

## TOGO'S DIARY ☙ SUMMER 1924

Usually we work for mining companies (gold was found in this part of Alaska in 1898), but Sepp says we have to be prepared to pull anything, so we train all winter and summer, on tracks or grass when there's no snow. We train so much we get to have huge meals each day—dried salmon, seal blubber, and sometimes even beaver-meat soup. Sepp even massages our muscles when we're tired. We respond with thank-you howls.

But in January 1925, we sled dogs would have to fetch
something even more important than gold—a cure
for a deadly disease.

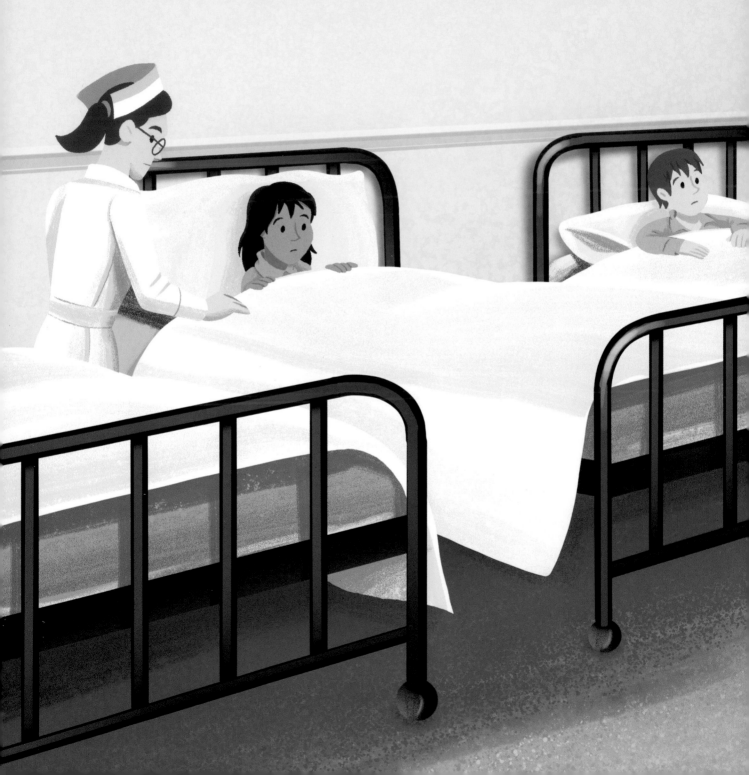

During the coldest, snowiest time of year, diphtheria had hit the town of Nome, Alaska. Diphtheria is an infection that makes it difficult to breathe. It was once the leading cause of childhood death in the world, before a vaccine to prevent it was developed.

Nome's only doctor didn't have enough of the serum, or medicine, to fight it. Many people were already sick—most of them children—and three had died by the time he sent a telegram to the US Public Health Service in Washington, DC, begging for help.

A package of small vials, or bottles, filled with the serum to treat diphtheria was wrapped in a quilt and placed in a crate at a hospital in Anchorage, Alaska. From there it was shipped by train to the farthest point it could go in the vast northern wilderness: a town called Nenana. Six hundred seventy-four miles separated Nenana from Nome, and there was only one way to travel it—dogsled.

## TOGO'S DIARY 🐾 JANUARY 27, 1925

This is it! Balto and I are going to be part of the Serum Race. Twenty teams of mushers—those are the sled drivers—and 150 dogs have been assigned to towns along the route in a relay race. Each musher will need to brave the blinding blizzard, strap the package to his sled, and race his dogs along the footpaths and dog trails until he reaches the next team in the relay. The route usually takes twenty-five days, but the serum will only last for SIX. And every day, more people are falling ill. We have to race faster than we have ever gone before!

The first musher and his nine-dog crew left Nenana
on January 27 at 9:00 p.m. and headed out into
the night. The weather was a howling fifty degrees
below zero and getting worse every minute.

It's not safe for dogs to run in
temperatures under forty below, but the
teams felt they had no choice. Every hour of delay
meant the illness could spread to more people.

Sepp and his pack, led by me, Togo, had to race 170 miles in the wrong direction just to get to the town where we would be picking up the serum. Then when we received the package, we had to turn around and race back across the most dangerous part of the journey, the shortcut across Norton Sound. The sound was the most direct route during winter, when it was frozen, but cracks in the ice made it scary to cross.

The organizers trusted Sepp with this hazardous part of the journey because he was known as the "King of the Trail." For years he had won racing trophies and awards. He had confidence and experience, but he also had me. Sepp called me the "best dog that ever traveled the Alaska trail." Aw, I'm blushing. Now it was time to put all those lead dog skills—speed, power, dependability, and endurance—to the test.

The snow was blinding, so I had to rely on my instincts and my knowledge of the trails and the ice, but we made it! We passed the package to the next relay team after a ninety-one-mile trip.

Here's where Balto joins the story. Another musher, Gunnar Kaasen, took Balto and twelve other dogs the final fifty-three miles of the journey. At one point the sled flipped over and the package flew off into a snowdrift!

But even with frostbitten fingers,
Kaasen found the serum, strapped it
back on, and raced to Nome.

After 674 miles and five and a half days,
the serum had reached its destination.

We received a hero's welcome when we all got back to Nome, but more importantly, the sick children all received the serum (once it had thawed!).

The town was saved.

## TOGO'S DIARY 🐾 1925

Most dog owners think that since I'm twelve years old, I should be retiring to spend the rest of my days lazy and warm in front of a fire. Not me! We've left home to travel throughout America, from Hollywood to New York. Everywhere we go, crowds cheer for the dogs who rescued a town. Balto got most of the fame for racing the final leg into Nome—he starred in movies and had a statue made of him— but now it's my turn in the spotlight.

Maybe we'll get tired of all these parades and
parties, but if we do, there's just one thing we'll
want to do—strap on a harness and get racing!

# Fact Sheet

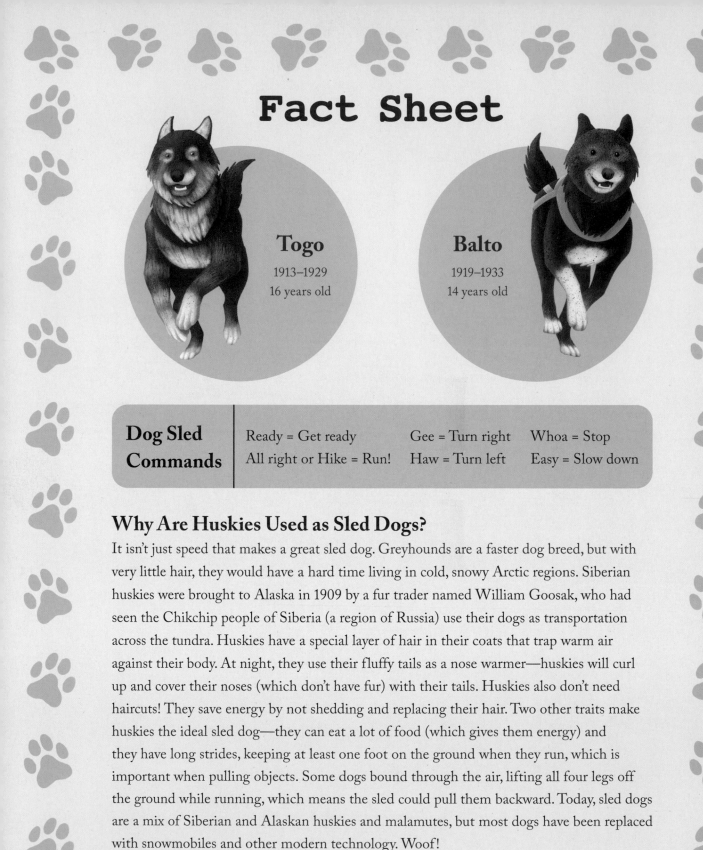

**Togo**

1913–1929

16 years old

**Balto**

1919–1933

14 years old

| **Dog Sled Commands** | Ready = Get ready | Gee = Turn right | Whoa = Stop |
|---|---|---|---|
| | All right or Hike = Run! | Haw = Turn left | Easy = Slow down |

## Why Are Huskies Used as Sled Dogs?

It isn't just speed that makes a great sled dog. Greyhounds are a faster dog breed, but with very little hair, they would have a hard time living in cold, snowy Arctic regions. Siberian huskies were brought to Alaska in 1909 by a fur trader named William Goosak, who had seen the Chikchip people of Siberia (a region of Russia) use their dogs as transportation across the tundra. Huskies have a special layer of hair in their coats that trap warm air against their body. At night, they use their fluffy tails as a nose warmer—huskies will curl up and cover their noses (which don't have fur) with their tails. Huskies also don't need haircuts! They save energy by not shedding and replacing their hair. Two other traits make huskies the ideal sled dog—they can eat a lot of food (which gives them energy) and they have long strides, keeping at least one foot on the ground when they run, which is important when pulling objects. Some dogs bound through the air, lifting all four legs off the ground while running, which means the sled could pull them backward. Today, sled dogs are a mix of Siberian and Alaskan huskies and malamutes, but most dogs have been replaced with snowmobiles and other modern technology. Woof!